DBT Workbook for Kids (Ages 6-10)

A Guide to Learn about Emotions to Regulate Anxiety and Stress (Self-Regulation Skills and Exercises)

D1523248

By

Chrissie Borg

The Fox Books

Loth Rozum
NEK
6/ 2023

Disclaimer Notice

This book is written and published independently. Please keep in mind that the material in this publication is solely for educational and entertaining purposes. All efforts have provided authentic, up-to-date, trustworthy, and comprehensive information. There are no express or implied assurances. The purpose of this book's material is to assist readers in having a better understanding of the subject matter. The activities, information, and exercises are provided solely for self-help information. This book is not intended to replace expert psychologists, legal, financial, or other guidance. If you require counseling, please get in touch with a qualified professional.

By reading this text, the reader accepts that the author will not be held liable for any damages, indirectly or directly, experienced due to the use of the information included herein, particularly, but not limited to, omissions, errors, or inaccuracies. As a reader, you are accountable for your decisions, actions, and consequences.

About the Author

Chrissie Borg is a professor and life coach with expert knowledge in Behavioral Psychology. She has extensive knowledge from ten years of working in the different fields of human Psychology, with hundreds of couples, women, and parents seeking her advice and using it to flourish in their lives.

She focuses on assisting couples in embracing compassion, connection, and good communication skills, arguing that intimate relationships require effort from both partners to work. She has a deep insight into what causes the couple's disputes and how to resolve them. Throughout her career, she has assisted hundreds of couples in improving their married life by working on their communication and conflict management skills.

She has provided Therapy to many individuals suffering from BPD to help them lead a useful life. Providing counseling and treatment to people suffering from mental disorders, helping couples and parents improve their family relations, time management, building confidence in women, and improving the quality of life through healthy habits are some of her favorite writing topics.

Contents

Chapter 2: Emotional Regulation....................53

Chapter 3: Distress Tolerance.......................72

Introduction

Children experience both good and terrible days, just like adults. We anticipate that a youngster will occasionally get angry, agitated, or impatient. But kids have high emotions all the time, and they could be angry or irritable nearly every day of the week. A youngster who experiences emotional overload frequently may act impulsively or have frequent outbursts of anger. If your child has regular outburst, you could be asking how to handle a child who has anger problems and whether there is really such a thing as child therapy. How do you recognize when a child's behavior calls for professional intervention?

You are not alone if you are unsure about where to start or what to do. There is hope, regardless of the reason of the behavior. Coping with difficult feelings and behaviors is not easy for the parents or the child.

Consider dialectical behavior treatment for children, also known as (DBT). DBT seeks to assist parents in supporting their children in developing beneficial coping mechanisms. Although DBT is a relatively new therapy option for kids, it is a good one. Children acquire DBT coping mechanisms with DBT for children (DBT-C) so they can manage intense emotions and take pleasure in their time with friends, family, and everything else that makes them happy.

You doubtless have many inquiries regarding DBT and whether it is appropriate for you and your child. We hope that by providing information about DBT in this book, we will encourage healing.

DBT is a version of child therapy that was altered to take into account the therapeutic requirements and developmental stages of children. Through a series of steps, DBT aims to teach coping mechanisms, alter harmful cognitive processes, and lessen emotional extremes. Clients are therefore better able to control their emotions, learn how to live in the moment, and deal with the underlying issue. Creating a strong living and pursuing self-fulfillment are further components of DBT. In contrast to other therapies, DBT aims to assist the client in striking a balance between tolerance and transformation.

Borderline personality disorder was the reason behind the development of DBT. Nevertheless, it is utilized to successfully treat patients with various diseases like mood disorders, eating disorders, anxiety, and attention deficit hyperactivity disorder (ADHD). Borderline personality disorder has been successfully treated with DBT.

To accommodate the developmental stages of preadolescent children, DBT has been updated. To address issues with emotion control and destructive behavior patterns, older kids and young adults may want to think about receiving regular DBT therapy.

DBT generally focuses on techniques that make kids and parents more conscious of their feelings and how those feelings affect their behavior. Children in a DBT program will also learn coping mechanisms and efficient ways of expressing their emotions and thoughts in stressful situations. A youngster can understand and apply the coping mechanisms and techniques presented by DBT.

For children to benefit the most from DBT treatment in the long run, they are unable to fully utilize DBT skills on their own and must have their parents' assistance. The DBT parent component prepares parents to serve as their child's counselor when treatment is complete. For a child to continue using DBT coping mechanisms, ongoing assistance is essential.

Parents need not be concerned; they will become fully informed throughout their child's treatment. For instance, parents will learn how to set an example for their children, how to foster a supportive environment, and how to encourage daily DBT practice. The parent element of DBT attempts to strengthen the bond between parents and children.

It is not at all simple to raise a child. Sometimes it might be difficult to determine whether a youngster needs assistance or is simply going through a phase. We are here to support you as a parent so that you don't have to face the difficulties of parenting a child on your own. Keeping in mind the basics and key points of child therapy and kids' emotions, this book is designed to assist kids as well as parents to fight back with the problems. This book covers the four important components of DBT including mindfulness and interpersonal effectiveness. Each chapter is full of engaging, entertaining, knowledge based and fun activities. Start reading this book, solve the worksheets, follow the exercises and explore more to get rid of your kids' emotional issues.

Hi Kids!

Hey kids! It is alright. Everyone feels different emotions and face different situations in life. What you have to be careful is not to let those emotions in your mind for longer. But if you feel like it is not in your control, try DBT therapy. Treatment is important and can be beneficial when started earlier. Here I will tell you a story of Diana about her mental suffering and how she overcame her problems through DBT Therapy.

Growing up, Diana did not feel easy. Her mother's severe sickness placed her in the hospital for extended periods of time when she was a little child. Early in life, she experienced significant anxiety, and she struggled to make friends at school. She eventually got an eating disorder, and at age 13, she started hurting herself. At the age of 15, Diana admits, "I had what you'd call a breakdown. I skipped school for the majority of the year." Long-term therapy for Diana had mainly consisted of unstructured talk therapy and medication. She was admitted to an adolescent section at a medical Centre that she described to be horrific and terrible and she started having suicidal thoughts. "Another patient assaulted me, and they did nothing," According to Diana, she started feeling more miserable than when she was discharged.

But afterwards, she turned to a DBT-trained therapist. She was enrolled by that clinician in a 28-day DBT "boot camp" for youngsters with emotions related disorders. For 28 days, she adds, "we studied and did DBT exercises all day, every day." Diana is doing quite well now, a year later. She considers some of the DBT techniques more useful than others, so she concentrates her efforts there. The three biggest ones for her are "distress tolerance, meditation, and emotional regulation abilities. The personal performance skills aren't very beneficial to me because I don't quarrel with others or even my parents."

In addition to the collection of coping mechanisms she has developed to deal with painful feelings, Diana heavily relies on journal cards, daily diaries that record her moods and feelings, what caused them, and how she reacted to them both negative and positive. She currently is 11 years old. To calm herself down, she uses breathing exercises.

DBT "changed her life," according to Diana 's father. But according to Diana, it's not quite that easy.

"I would say that a brilliant therapist, DBT workbooks, and breathing exercises saved my life".

Stress and Anxiety in Kids

Any situation where a child must adjust or change can cause them to experience childhood stress. Positive changes, like beginning a new activity, can sometimes generate stress, but these are less prevalent than bad ones, like illness or a death in the family. A child's reaction to a bad shift in their lives may be stress. Stress can be beneficial in moderation. However, too much stress can have an impact on a child's emotions, thoughts, and behavior.

As they mature and develop, kids learn how to handle stress. A youngster will experience stress from many difficult situations that an adult can handle. As a result, even minor changes might have an effect on a child's sense of security.

Children experience stress from pain, injury, disease, and other changes. Physical or behavioral changes are frequent indicators of stress and anxiety in children. According to their age, unique personalities, and coping mechanisms, children react to stress in different ways, which can lead many parents to ignore the underlying problems that might be influencing their child's behavior.

It is critical for parents to be aware of the symptoms of childhood stress and to investigate potential reasons. While parents can usually assist kids in managing stress and anxiety, certain kids may develop anxiety disorders and should seek professional assistance.

Children's Anxiety Symptoms

Children frequently lack the ability to express their genuine or imagined stressful circumstances, making it difficult for them to understand their own anxiety. Parents may be unclear as to whether various physical and behavioral symptoms are indications of anxiety or a medical issue as a result of this. So, I am mentioning common signs of stress and anxiety in children.

1. Emotional or Behavioral

It is crucial for caregivers to understand that these behavioral and emotional disorders may be linked to emotions of worry. Anxiety can drive children to behave out in ways that might be annoying or puzzling to parents. Following are a few typical behavioral indicators of stress and anxiety:

- Behavioral alterations include irritability, hostility, a quick temper, or clinginess
- Forming an anxious habit, such as biting one's nails
- Having trouble focusing
- Fears
- Having problems at school
- Collecting seemingly insignificant objects
- Refusing to attend school
- Isolation from friends or relatives

2. Physical

Physical symptoms are another way that stress and worry can show up. A few of these indicators include:

- Bedwetting
- Complaints of migraines or stomachaches
- A change in or an increase in appetite
- Additional physical signs
- Issues with sleep or nightmares

Consider whether these symptoms regularly appear before or after particular activities and whether any physical symptoms, such as discomfort, fever, rash, or diarrhea, could indicate a medical issue.

Common Causes of Stress in Children

Children's anxiety and tension can have an external cause, such a problem at school, a change in the family, or a disagreement with a friend. Internal pressures and emotions, such as the desire to perform well in school or fit in with classmates, can also contribute to a child's anxious feelings. Typical reasons why kids experience stress include:

Academic Pressure: Wanting to perform well in school causes anxiety in many children. Children who are frightened of making errors or who are fearful of failing at anything often experience academic pressure.

Major Life Events: Your child's sense of security can be shaken by significant life changes like divorce, a family crisis, relocating, or the introduction of a new sibling, which can cause bewilderment and anxiety. A youngster may feel threatened and envious when they get a new sibling, for instance. An unexpected death in the family can cause worry, sorrow, and even fear of death.

Bullying: Bullying is a significant issue for many kids. It might cause bodily harm and might either be subtle or evident. Children who are bullied frequently experience embarrassment about being the target, and they may hide the abuse from teachers or parents out of concern that doing so will expose their alleged flaws.

Catastrophic News Event: Images and headlines from terrorism, natural disasters, and violent crimes can be unsettling to young viewers. Children may worry that there is something horrible that might occur to them or someone they care about when they watch and hear about awful news occurrences.

Parental Instability: Concerns about money and employment, marital strife, and parental restlessness can leave youngsters feeling hopeless and helpless despite their desire to assist.

Popularity: Separation anxiety is a prevalent issue for younger grade school students. Most youngsters want to be liked and fit in with other kids as they get older; this pressure to do so can be excruciating. Once children start grade school, cliques and a sense of exclusion frequently start to be a problem.

Overly Busy Schedules: Constantly rushing from one activity to the next might be highly stressful for the kids who often require some quiet downtime.

Scary Films or Journals: Fictional tales can also make kids feel upset or anxious. Thrilling, violent, or upsetting book passages or movie sequences frequently have an impact on children.

Now, use this story to tell your kids that there are many other things to enjoy rather than worrying or stressing about fancy things.

Once, a group of school students who got quite successful in their careers made the decision to meet one of their school teachers. They all visited their former school teacher together one day.

When they first met the teacher, everyone began to talk about their lives and jobs, but this conversation quickly devolved into grumbling and stress-related topics.

After some time, the teacher went to the kitchen to get coffee for the students. He came back with a big pot of coffee and a selection of cups, including expensive, porcelain, glass, crystal, and plastic.

He asked his students to help themselves to the coffee after setting the coffee pot and mugs on the table. Students had cups of coffee in their hands after selection.

"The plain or inexpensive cups are on the table in their place, while all the expensive-looking cups have been taken", the teacher remarked. It's natural for each of you to desire what's best for yourself, but you can't understand that this is the root of all your issues and stress.

"You are all aware that the cup itself does not improve the flavor of the coffee", he continued. All of you carefully chose the best cups even though what you really wanted was only coffee to drink, not the cup.

Moral of the Story: When we focus on the fancy looking things and compare ourselves with others, we lose the sense of happiness and eventually become stressed. Sometimes, this anxiety or stress comes from embarrassing situations, hurtful event, fears etc. But focusing on the good and setting the future goals to believe in yourself is what you really need. Gratitude is the big thing in life and no matter what will be the situation, do not let your guards down. Believe in yourself and don't lose hope.

DBT FOR KIDS

Kids and preadolescents who suffer from strong emotions and behaviors can benefit from dialectical behavior therapy (DBT), an evidence-based therapy. DBT helps families and children by utilizing a variety of therapeutic modalities, such as individual therapy, skill development, working directly with families, and round-the-clock coaching over the phone. Family members frequently describe kids and preadolescents who gain from DBT as:

- Extreme or "sticky" thinking, which is the tendency to believe that everything is either wonderful or terrible.
- Excessive behavior, including hurting oneself or others, damaging property, and making snap judgments without considering the ramifications.
- Extreme emotional sensitivity, self-criticism for seemingly insignificant things, feeling their emotions more intensely than their siblings and friends, and difficulty letting go of unfavorable emotions are all signs of extreme emotional sensitivity.

Parents and instructors have been known to "walk on eggshells" around them to prevent emotional and behavioral outbursts around these kids. Through a structured approach, DBT helps children and preadolescents deal with these problems so that they and their families can think more flexibly and control their strong emotions and behaviors. DBT also teaches kids and preadolescents how to form and maintain healthy connections with other individuals.

Children who suffer emotional dysregulation and related behavioral decontrol were the target population for DBT for Children (DBT-C), which was created to address their therapeutic needs. Compared to their peers, these kids experience emotions considerably more intensely and differently. Little things bother them, and their emotions can become so intense that they are verbally or physically aggressive. Sometimes it could seem like these kids are trying to play with people's emotions and buttons. However, the child's explosive actions may be the finest coping mechanism they have for their powerful feelings.

Additionally, since these actions are frequently rewarded, they could persist. It's possible that the environment isn't prepared to handle the difficulties these kids bring, and "good enough parenting" might not be enough to handle these demands. The environment frequently invalidates a child's needs because it cannot fully meet them, further destabilizing the youngster. A more unstable youngster puts greater pressure on the surroundings to react appropriately, further invalidating the situation. Over time, this transaction can cause psychopathology to emerge. According to research, these kids are more likely to experience alcohol and drug abuse issues, suicidal behavior and non-suicidal subconscious, melancholy, stress, and psychological issues as they age into adolescence and adulthood. The main objectives of DBT are to teach these kids effective problem-solving and adaptive coping techniques and teach their parents how to foster an environment that is accepting of the change.

If the above signs are similar to your kids' symptoms, continue reading and you will get the plenty of activities and exercises to make your kids' life normal and happy.

But...

How do you believe that DBT will really help your kid?

Let's look at some success stories of DBT.

Case Study 1

Jennie, a single Caucasian girl at her 12, is seen as a client with clinical complexity. Both major depression and a self-harm are listed as her diagnosis.

Over the past three years, Jennie received outpatient and intensive outpatient mental health care. Through it all, her family had been encouraging but after some time, they felt helpless as Jennie battled her addiction to self-harm. She had started to shut down and distance herself from her family due to her severe sadness.

However, there had been times when Jennie and her parents had fought and disagreed. Regarding Jennie's disobedient behavior, Jennie 's parents had become extremely concerned and anxious. Due to her desperation, Jennie had gotten to the point where she could not get out of bed and was continuously cursing her parents. The parents of Jennie kept looking into dual diagnosis inpatient institutions that provided evidence-based therapies.

While they awaited hearing about Jennie 's eligibility for admittance to an inpatient institution, Jennie 's parents arranged for her to undergo a thorough psychiatric evaluation. An inpatient program for young girls ages 9 to 12 accepted Jennie and admitted her.

Dialectical Behavior Therapy was used in the treatment plan (DBT). The first step in applying DBT was to identify the problematic behavioral patterns that were the root of Jennie 's problems and kept her from thriving in all areas of her life.

These patterns threatened Jennie 's functionality, care, and quality of life, which were methodically targeted by a hierarchy of behavior.

The foundation for comprehending Jennie 's issues was DBT. Together with the suggestions from the complete psychological evaluation, the DBT framework and treatment methods helped

21

produce a customized treatment plan. Due to her severe sadness at the time and her difficulty adjusting to the well-organized days in the environment, Jennie initially had difficulty. She spent more time with the counselor to reiterate her commitment to DBT therapy and the goals she had established at the start of treatment.

Case Study 2

(Henry will tell you his story)

My name is Henry. I have been studying DBT for six or seven months. I've seen numerous ways in which DBT is benefiting me. I did not have healthy problem-solving skills before beginning DBT. I've learned several useful skills from DBT. I've gotten better at identifying when I'm anxious, worried, or depressed. I've been practicing various techniques for self-control till I can feel my palms relax and my muscles loosen.

I don't have to act on my emotions immediately. I am able to put the issue on hold for a bit and return to it once I've calmed down. I've also discovered that I have choices. When I feel threatened or disregarded, I can choose how I want to react. I've discovered that sometimes the "opposite action" to how I want to react might improve things. I've realized that my mind can only focus on one subject at once. I work on maintaining my attention and handling the current circumstance. I've grown to love myself and open up to other people a lot more. Sometimes I have to work on not passing judgment, but I'm improving.

Because it has prompted me to reflect more on my environment and self, mindfulness is something I enjoy. Now that I can see the larger picture, it's easier for me to make choices that won't lead to further issues in the future. Even though I try to force myself to go, I occasionally find it difficult to attend gatherings. Sometimes I can get knowledge from the experiences and stories of others. When the leaders teach the skills, I attempt to imagine how that skill might benefit me. This way, I can learn from them as well.

I used to be quite timid when I had a question. I've learned how to ask and receive responses to the questions that have been on my mind because of DBT. I won't have to fret or ponder about anything after that. I've had the guts to ask, thanks to DBT, and frequently the responses have been more helpful than I had anticipated.

I hope these case studies have assured you about the success of DBT therapy in kids. Let's move forward to treatment worksheets and exercises.

Chapter 1: Interpersonal Relationships

A relationship is like a large, lush tree. A tree needs a strong root system to support and nourish it. The tree's size, strength, and development increase as the roots grow. The tree may even start to bear fruit! Your connections with other people have roots, just like a tree. A good relationship has strong roots to flourish. Dialectical behavioral therapy (DBT) teaches specific techniques to kids to establish solid foundations and create or sustain healthy relationships with your kids. Building and maintaining wholesome relationships is one of the interpersonal success abilities taught in DBT. People who have had positive relationships across their lives frequently, come naturally with these abilities. DBT has broken down these characteristics into different skills. Anyone can benefit from learning these techniques, but those who have endured trauma or an attachment disorder find it especially useful. The DBT skill is especially beneficial for kids to strengthening their relationship bonds.

Interpersonal Effectiveness

First of all, you need to understand what are the things that get in the way of healthy relationships. Read and teach your kids about the relationship facts.

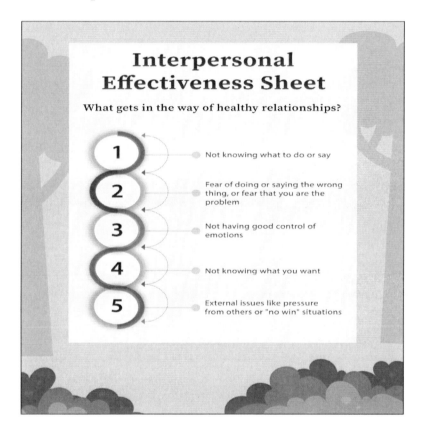

Skills Assessment Handout

It is a good idea to assess your kids' present level of interpersonal skills with interpersonal communication abilities handout before attempting to enhance them. This handout's assessment can be useful. Ask your kids and fill out the questionnaire. You can simply analyze this questionnaire by comparing scores from each question.

There are 29 skills listed on this page, including:

- Identify yourself
- Hearing what others are saying while listening
- Showing interest in others by listening
- Retorting to compliments
- Taking action in response to criticism
- Self-disclosure when necessary

You are required to rate your kids' performance for each ability using the following rubric and a scale from 1 to 5:

1: I'm not particularly good at that skill.

2 - I'm not good.

3 – I Occasionally do well.

4 - I generally do well

5 - I always do well.

Establishing a baseline is important if you want to improve your communication abilities. It is much simpler to spot improvements if you have a baseline to go back to!

1.	Identify yourself	1	2	3	4	5
2.	Hearing what others are saying while listening	1	2	3	4	5
3.	Showing interest in others by listening	1	2	3	4	5

4.	expressing emotions	1	2	3	4	5
5.	Managing rage and antagonism	1	2	3	4	5
6.	retorting to compliments	1	2	3	4	5
7.	reacting to anxious expression	1	2	3	4	5
8.	Taking action in response to criticism	1	2	3	4	5
9.	Managing apathy and displays of disinterest	1	2	3	4	5
10.	Managing conversational pauses	1	2	3	4	5
11.	respecting the emotions of others	1	2	3	4	5
12.	Providing information and advice on emotional problems or situations	1	2	3	4	5
13.	looking for clarity	1	2	3	4	5
14.	posing open-ended inquiries	1	2	3	4	5
15.	awaiting responses	1	2	3	4	5
16.	The topic of the conversation is changed	1	2	3	4	5
17.	demonstrating support	1	2	3	4	5

18.	Self-disclosure when necessary	1	2	3	4	5
19.	raising the stakes of a conversation	1	2	3	4	5
20.	lowering the seriousness of a discourse	1	2	3	4	5
21.	a summary of what has been mentioned	1	2	3	4	5
22.	sustaining a person's interest and focus	1	2	3	4	5
23.	concluding discussions in a positive manner	1	2	3	4	5
24.	Ability to plan	1	2	3	4	5
25.	Managing time	1	2	3	4	5
26	Conflict resolution	1	2	3	4	5
28.	completing tasks	1	2	3	4	5
29.	Identify yourself	1	2	3	4	5

There is another simple activity for your kids to assess their skills. Follow the instructions given.

Skills Assessment Handout

Name: _____ **Date:** _____

Please circle the easy button if that skill is easy for you to complete. If you think you need some help to do the skill circle the help button.

Skill	Easy	Help
Keeping desk or locker organized	easy	help
Keeping track of daily assignment	easy	help
Handwriting notes in a timely manner	easy	help
Neatly writing notes	easy	help
Writing out math problems or numbers	easy	help
Opening locker	easy	help
Changing classes	easy	help

Try Not to Listen Activity

It is a group activity for school teacher. Parents can also customize it according to available resources.

Request that the students pair up for a task. As long as the other person is not listening, each individual will have a turn speaking for two minutes about whatever topic they choose. Let's call them A and B. A speaks for two minutes, and B doesn't appear to be listening by remaining silent. Then they switch places, and B is in charge.

Participants who attempt to speak for two minutes typically run out of things to say before that time. It is challenging to continue when no one is paying attention to you. Since this is a playful opening to the activity, it doesn't matter whether it devolves into amusing chaos—the points will still be made.

Ask A and B how it felt not to be listened to after they have each had a turn speaking, then discuss and record their instant thoughts on the board or flipchart.

The solutions they are likely to offer are represented by the list below:

- Frustrated
- Angry/cross/livid
- It doesn't matter
- It was tedious that I had to say.
- I dried up and couldn't continue.
- I felt unimportant.

Then, please inquire what actions they saw the person exhibiting when they weren't being listened to.

The list of typical responses is as follows:

- Head lowered (looking at the floor)
- There is no eye contact.

- Observing the floor and ceiling
- Crossed legs and folded arms
- No expression or boredom
- Yawning/whistling/scratching
- Preoccupied
- Nothing exchanged.

While it is obvious that this exercise exaggerates the experience of talking to someone who isn't paying attention, it might nevertheless be useful for those who lack social awareness or have poor social skills to watch their behavior in social situations.

It is simple to engage in active listening during interactions, but it can be challenging to remember to do so while also engaging in all desired behaviors. Participants will be able to recognize and recall the traits of a good listener after practicing this.

Sabotage Exercise

Another enjoyable exercise highlights positive interpersonal habits by using negative interpersonal behaviors.

This activity should be done in a group that is sizable enough to be divided into at least 2 or 3 teams of 4 to 5 people.

Give each group a 10-minute time limit to brainstorm ideas, discuss them, and compile a list of every possible technique to sabotage a collective project. Anything they can conceive is OK as long as it is disruptive enough to derail a team task completely.

Gather the bigger group once more and compare answers once each group has a sizable list of ways to sabotage a group assignment. In front of the room, write them down on the flip board, chalkboard, or whiteboard.

Reorganize the groups after that and give them the task of creating a 5- to 10-point agreement outlining the rules for productive group work. To find good ideas, group members should use the sabotage suggestions (i.e., what not to do for effective group work).

A group might suggest "communicate with other members of the group often" as a rule for productive group work, for instance, if they listed "do not interact with any of the other members of the group" as a means to undermine the group assignment.

Participants will learn through this activity what makes for a good experience in a group while also getting an opportunity to enjoy one themselves.

Strengths and Weaknesses

When it comes to getting things done, groups have one major benefit over individuals: they can balance the group by making up for each person's flaws and complementing their strengths.

In this exercise, group members will critically reflect on their strengths and flaws and the weaknesses and strengths of their fellow group members and the group as a whole.

Give this activity a try by asking the group to consider the positives and negatives of each group member. Encourage them to talk openly about their flaws while still being kind to one another.

Make each group consider how these will impact group dynamics after each team has developed a solid list of each member's strengths and shortcomings. What qualities will facilitate productive group interactions? Which flaws could potentially complicate group interactions?

Finally, ask each team to debate the elements of the "ideal" team. Is it preferable to have individuals with diverse personalities, talents, and skills or those with more similar traits? What are the benefits and drawbacks of every team type?

Participants will understand what makes a great squad, how various personalities connect, and how to adapt behavior, group behavior, or expectations to accommodate the various personalities and skill sets of others through this conversation. Use worksheets given below to write strengths and weaknesses.

My Strengths and Weaknesses

Things I am good at...

1

2

3

Compliments I have received...

1

2

3

What I like about my appearance...

1

2

3

Challenges I have overcome...

1

2

3

I have helped others by...

1

2

3

Things that make me unique...

1

2

3

What I value the most...

1

2

3

Times I have made others happy...

1

2

3

Strengths & Weaknesses

Date:

My Top Ten Strengths:

1	6
2	7
3	8
4	9
5	10

My Top Ten Weaknesses:

1	6
2	7
3	8
4	9
5	10

One of my weaknesses that is now a strength is:

One weakness I'd like to make a strength is:

Count the Squares Game

This game is beneficial for teachers. Parents can also customize it. The group connection and communication that this game promotes are exciting and enjoyable.

All you require is a PowerPoint presentation, an image having number of squares merge with one another, and a board or wall at the front of the room.

Give each group member a few minutes to count the number of squares in the diagram and record their result for the first step. They should carry out this action in silence.

The next step is having each team member announce how many squares they counted. Put them in writing on the board.

Now tell each person to pick a partner and have them count the squares once more. When calculating the number of squares, they can converse with each other but not with anybody else.

Once they're done, ask each pair to reveal their number.

After that, encourage the participants to divide into groups of 4 to 5 people each and count the squares once more. Take note of the numbers each group counted once more after completion.

There will probably have been at least one group determining the right number of squares. Ask this group to explain how they reached to the correct answer to the other participants.

Finally, have a group conversation about how group synergy works and how additional people joining the effort to fix the issue likely caused the numbers to increase until they eventually reached the correct answer.

In addition to practicing working in groups or pairs, participants will learn the value of effective group communication while doing this activity.

Non-Verbal Introduction Game

Parents, counsellors and teachers can benefit from this activity. Meeting new people and presenting them to the group is the focus of this entertaining game.

To take advantage of the chance to meet each group member, you should organize this game for the first day of therapy, training, or another activity.

Pair up each group member with the person seated next to them. Tell them to make introductions and share something unique or fascinating about themselves.

Bring attention to the broader group once each pair has been introduced and learned something fascinating about the other person.

Inform the group members that they must present their partners to the group, but there is a restriction: neither words nor props are permitted! Each partner must only use actions to introduce the other partner.

This game is not only a fantastic way to get to know new people, but it is also a fun method for group members to appreciate both the value of nonverbal communication and the utility of oral communication.

If you have the time, you may lead a group in a conversation about nonverbal clues, behavioral indicators, and the importance of gaining feedback from the individuals you speak with.

Verbal Communication

I have some cards for verbal communication tips. Teach kids about the key terms mentioned in cards for excellent verbal communication.

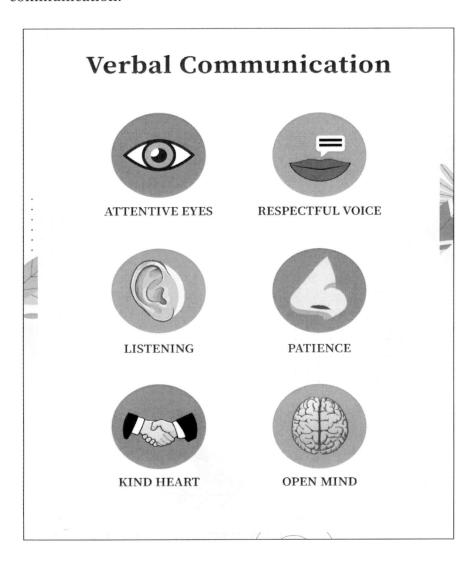

Negotiation

Negotiation is an important life skill for kids. Use this activity to teach negotiation skills.

Negotiate

Most situations that lead to anger could be resolved with effective negotiation. To negotiate effectively, try the following:

1. Maintain good body language, eye contact and <u>listening skills.</u>

2. Let each side clarify their position or wants by using I statements.

3. Ask for a compromise and be prepared to compromise.

4. Discuss a win/win situation where both individuals agree on setting.

Role play the following situations using your negotiation skills:

1. Both individuals want the same item.

2. One individual has taken your device to play with without asking and doesn't want to give it back.

3. Both individuals can't agree on which show to watch.

4. One individual won't let you participate in group work.

5. Somebody knocked an item of yours over and won't pick it up.

6. Somebody is excluding you from something you want to do.

7. You have been lied to and your friend is denying it.

8. Rude things are being said about you by your friend on social media.

9. You got into trouble for something you did not do.

10. Your friend keeps yelling and insulting you.

11. You both want same device.

12. You are getting a new pet but your sibling wants a dog and you want a cat. You can't get both.

13. You have broken your sibling's favorite toy and your sibling is very mad.

Communication Cards

Communication Cards

Directions: Cut out these communication cards and allow your child to choose their preferred method of communicating with friends, family, and peers.

I can give a hug.

I can smile.

I can wave.

I can give a kiss.

I can point to a picture.

I can give a high five.

Problem-Solving

Use these worksheets to develop problem solving skills in your kids.

PROBLEM
SOLVING WORKSHEET

1. What was the problem? _____

_____

2. When? _____

Where? _____

With whom? _____

_____

3. What positive choices could you have made?

_____

_____

_____

3. What will you earn?

_____

PROBLEM SOLVING

When an event happens, what do you think will affect what you feel and what you do?

Situations

Describe the situation:
_____
_____
_____
_____

Thoughts

What were your thoughts?
_____
_____
_____

Feelings

How did you feel?
_____
_____
_____

Behavior

What were your behaviors (how did you react?):
_____
_____
_____

Outcome

What was the outcome?
_____
_____
_____

PROBLEM SOLVING

What problem is bothering you?

Think of 3 (or more) **possible solutions** to your problem	What are the **advantages** of this solutions?	What are the **disadvantages** of this solution?	Which is the **best** solution?
1.			
2.			
3.			

44

Decision-Making

These decision-making worksheets are a great source of learning for kids.

DECISION MAKING

3 good choices I would like to
make this week...

1) _____

_____

2) _____

_____

3) _____

_____

I predict my future to look like this if
I make these choices...

Solution brainstorming will help your kid to try different solutions for problem.

Name _____   Date _____

Solution Brainstorming

Directions: Follow the prompts to brainstorm solutions to a decision you are facing. Assess each possible outcome and consequences, then choose a solution! Check in later and note the outcomes of your choice and whether or not you were correct in your guesses.

Decision / Problem:

Solution 1	Solution 2	Solution 3
List 3 good things that can happen	List 3 good things that can happen	List 3 good things that can happen
List 3 not good things that can happen	List 3 not good things that can happen	List 3 not good things that can happen
How would these things make you feel?	How would these things make you feel?	How would these things make you feel?

The solution I will choose is... _____

The result of my choice was... _____
_____
_____

DECISION MAKING
Rate Yourself

Need to Work on it.........OK.......................Average............................Good.......................Excellent

1   **2**   **3**   **4**   **5**

What is your score for decision making?_____

Provide an example of a decision you made that was in the best interest of yourself and others:

_____

_____

_____

_____

_____

_____

What good decisions have you made about your own behaviors? _____

_____

_____

What does it mean to be a responsible decision maker ? _____

_____

_____

_____

_____

The Three Stages of Mind

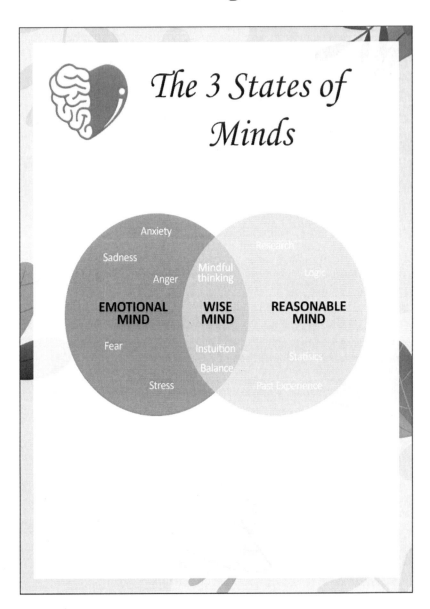

The 3 States of Minds

Anxiety

Sadness

Research

Anger

Mindful thinking

Logic

EMOTIONAL MIND

WISE MIND

REASONABLE MIND

Fear

Instuition

Statistics

Balance

Stress

Past Experience

Assertiveness

There are some statements given below. Ask kids to choose the assertive statements.

Being Assertive

Asserttive communication means standing up for yourself and sharing how you feel in a respectful manner! Place a check next to the examples of assertive communication.

Share why you think each example is or isn't a good example of someone being assertive!

-Cody asks, "Wyatt, can you please stop throwing the ball at me?"

-Diane pushes Ryan because he called her a bad name.

-Cheyenne says, "No. I don't like it when you do that. Please, Stop."

-Chris calls Bo a "chicken brain" because he's mad at him.

-Ian is mad at Hector for making fun of him, but he doesn't say anything to him.

-Tom is angry at his brother, so he sneaks in his room and breaks his toy.

-Francis doesn't let Vivian play his game because he's mad at her.

-Carol says, "I need you to please stop calling me names behind my back".

-Joann tells Brenda that she's the "worst friend in the world!"

-Paul pulls Eva to the side and asks her to be nicer to him.

-Sally is mad at Asher, so she counts to 10 before expressing her feelings.

-Darnell says, "I'm tired of you picking on me. It hurts my feelings."

-Brett tells Josh, "I'm giving you 10 seconds to run before I hit you!"

DEARMAN

DEARMAN

Sometimes interacting and having relations with people can be difficult. In situations that require confrontation it is important to make sure that you present yourself as assertive but not aggressive or disagreeable. Use **DEARMAN** to help you prepare for your difficult situation you are facing:

Describe. As objectively (without bias or judgement) as possible, describe the situation.

_____

_____

Express. Express how you are affected by this situation. How does the situation make you feel? Remember, keep the focus on the "I".

I feel: _____

Assert. Make your thoughts and expectations known. What do you think about situation?

_____

_____

Reinforce. Explain why do you think the way you do and why do you want what you want? Explain how what you are asking for will benefit you.

_____

_____

Mindful. Be mindful about how your feelings can influence your thoughts and communication skills. Be sure to avoid invalidating others or letting your emotions fuel your participation in the conversation.

_____

_____

Appear Confident. Remember that your presentation is important. Things like body language and tone can make a big difference in how your message is received. What can you do to ensure you apear confident but not confrontational?

_____

_____

Negotiate. Sometimes with difficult situations, there needs to be a compromise. In most circumstances compromise is possible. In what ways can you compromise, or negotiate terms in which both parties benefit?

_____

_____

_____

Chapter 2: Emotional Regulation

Emotion regulation is another component of dialectical behavior therapy (DBT), which teaches clients how to control strong, overpowering emotions while enhancing their positive ones. Three objectives are covered in this module:

- Recognize one's feelings
- Lessen emotional sensitivity
- Lessen the emotional pain

Understanding that unpleasant feelings are not harmful or something that must be avoided is a key component of emotion control. Although they are a natural part of life, there are ways to recognize them before letting them go, preventing one from becoming ruled by them.

Clients who are extremely sensitive to emotions frequently get through the cycles that start with an occurrence that sets off unwarrantedly negative thoughts. These feelings then cause an excessive or negative emotional reaction, resulting in disastrous behavioral decisions. More unpleasant feelings like shame and self-loathing come after the damaging behavior. Emotional regulation skills come into help when your emotions and feelings are going off from track. Use the worksheets and exercises given in this chapter to help your kids manage their emotions.

Emotion Regulation Goals Sheet

Emotional Regulation Sheet

Share examples of when you've experienced any of these feelings!

A time I felt HAPPY was when _____
_____

A time I felt ANGRY was when _____
_____

A time I felt DISAPPOINTED was when _____
_____

A time I felt NERVOUS was when _____
_____

A time I felt EMBARRASSED was when _____
_____

A time I felt CONFUSED was when _____
_____

A time I felt SAD was when _____
_____

Swap your Bad Habits

To manage emotions, it is important to manage your daily activities. Follow the chart.

SWAP YOUR BAD HABITS

HABIT TO CHANGE	WHAT IT GIVES ME	NEW HABIT!
Wake up & grab phone	Feeling of connection	Journal & drink tea
Skipping breakfast	Sense of control	Drink a nutritious smoothie
Spending money on things I don't need	Boost of mood	Put extra money towards a dream vacation
Binge watching Netflix after work	Relaxation and pleasure	Workout for 30 minutes at home
Snacking when I'm not hungry	Distracts my mind from work	Meditate for 5 minutes

Gratitude

Gratitude

I am grateful for my family because.... _____
_____

Something good that happened this week... _____
_____

I am grateful for my friendship with... _____ because... _____
_____

I am grateful for who I am because... _____
_____

Something silly that I am grateful for... _____
_____

Something else I am grateful for... _____
_____

PAUSE

Parents will help kids for this activity.

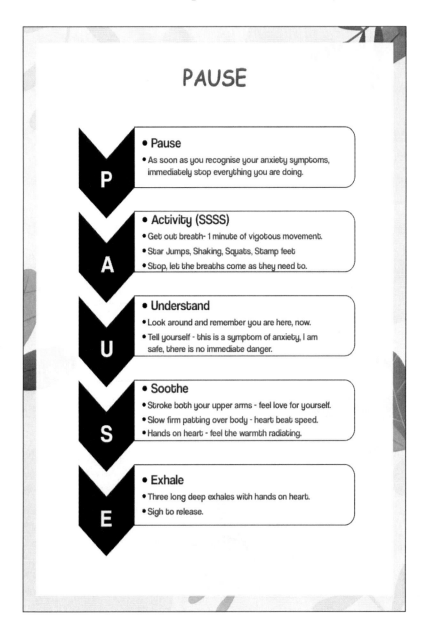

PAUSE

P • Pause
  • As soon as you recognise your anxiety symptoms, immediately stop everything you are doing.

A • Activity (SSSS)
  • Get out breath- 1 minute of vigotous movement.
  • Star Jumps, Shaking, Squats, Stamp feet
  • Stop, let the breaths come as they need to.

U • Understand
  • Look around and remember you are here, now.
  • Tell yourself - this is a symptom of anxiety, I am safe, there is no immediate danger.

S • Soothe
  • Stroke both your upper arms - feel love for yourself.
  • Slow firm patting over body - heart beat speed.
  • Hands on heart - feel the warmth radiating.

E • Exhale
  • Three long deep exhales with hands on heart.
  • Sigh to release.

Feeling Faces

Ask kids to rate their feelings on the given scale by considering different situations in mind.

My Emotional Cup

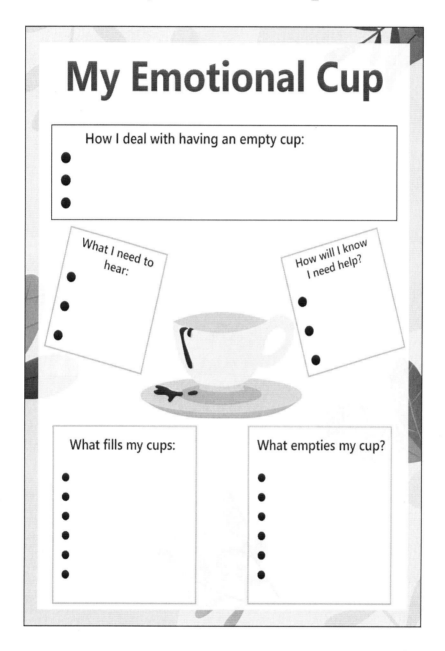

My Emotional Cup

How I deal with having an empty cup:
-
-
-

What I need to hear:
-
-
-

How will I know I need help?
-
-
-

What fills my cups:
-
-
-
-
-
-

What empties my cup?
-
-
-
-
-
-

Radical Acceptance

Radical Acceptance

- Accept what is-acknowledge reality

- Figure out what we can control and what we can't

- Look at our situation from a nonjudgement perspective-stick to the facts!

- Stop fighting reality

- Learn how to live in the present moment despite our pain

Situation to be accepted: _____

If you feel that this a big situation that is too difficult to work with, break it down into smaller chunks. This will help to make it more manageable. Complete this worksheet for each one, and practice radically accepting each of the smaller situations separately. If applicable, what are the smaller pieces within the whole situation that need to be accepted?

_____   _____

_____   _____

Choose one of these to work with: _____

Why is it important to accept this situation?

_____

_____

What could be different in your life if you accept this situation?

_____

_____

Rate your current level of acceptance from 0 to 10.

(0= no of acceptance, 10= complete radical acceptance) _____

The Wheel of Choice

Cut and paste this wheel in your kid's room. Whenever he feels down, spin and play.

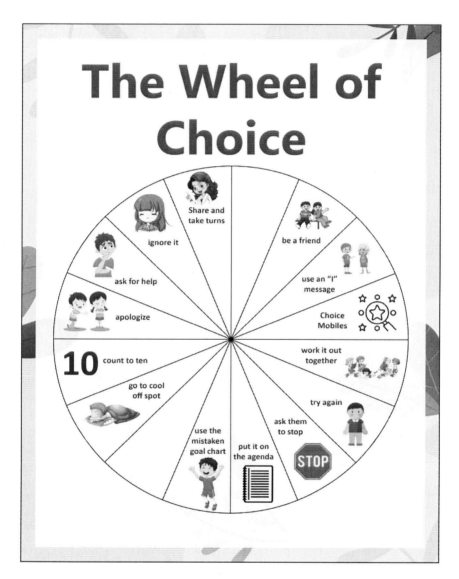

Does this Look Familiar?

Ask kids when they feel helpless or down, how do their body parts react?

Anger Management Dice Game

Parents need to make a list of six mindful activities. Whenever your kid will be feeling angry or upset, ask him to roll the dice and try the activity when dice gives the number. Use the worksheet below.

ACCEPTS

Help your kids to understand why ACCEPT skill is necessary to learn. Use the image below to create a situation related to points.

ACCEPTS

Skill helps us distract:

* ACTIVITIES
* CONTRIBUTING TO OTHERS
* COMPARISON
* EMOTIONS (OPPOSITE)
* PUSHING AWAY
* THOUGHTS
* SENSATIONS

Your Self-Talk

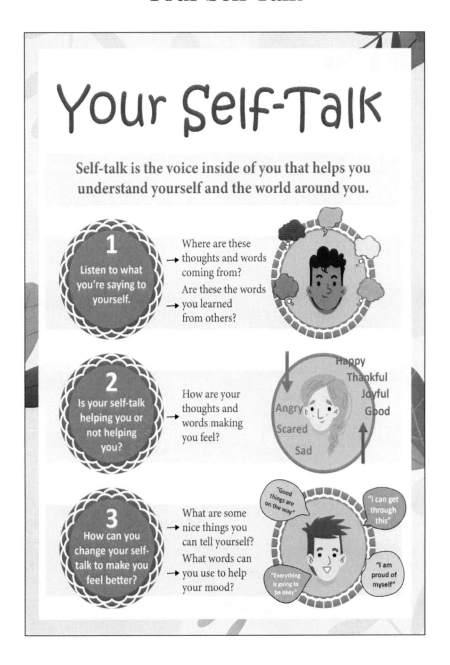

Your Self-Talk

Self-talk is the voice inside of you that helps you understand yourself and the world around you.

1 Listen to what you're saying to yourself.

→ Where are these thoughts and words coming from?

→ Are these the words you learned from others?

2 Is your self-talk helping you or not helping you?

→ How are your thoughts and words making you feel?

Happy
Thankful
Joyful
Good
Angry
Scared
Sad

3 How can you change your self-talk to make you feel better?

→ What are some nice things you can tell yourself?

→ What words can you use to help your mood?

"Good things are on the way"

"I can get through this"

"Everything is going to be okay"

"I am proud of myself"

Sitting in my Chair

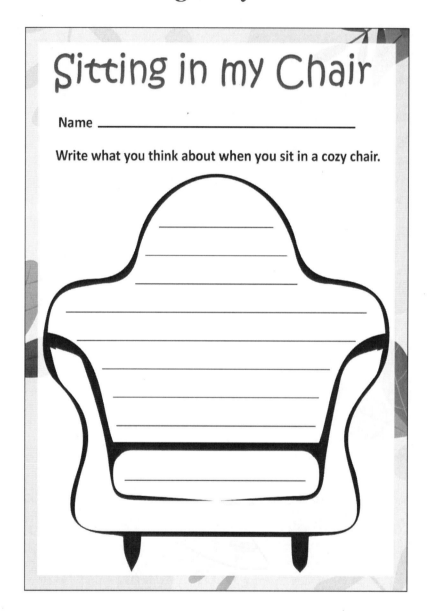

Sitting in my Chair

Name _____

Write what you think about when you sit in a cozy chair.

Acts of Self-Care

Five Things That I Like About Myself

Chapter 3: Distress Tolerance

Distress tolerance techniques used in dialectical behavior therapy (DBT) address the tendency of stress for some people who find it difficult to cope with negative emotions. Low-tolerance individuals may become overwhelmed by even small amounts of stress and exhibit negative behaviors. The distress tolerance component of DBT teaches clients that there will be instances when pain cannot be avoided and that the best course of action is to learn to tolerate and accept suffering. Many conventional treatment approaches place a strong emphasis on avoiding uncomfortable situations.

Radical acceptance is a crucial component of distress tolerance. When a person cannot change the circumstance, this refers to accepting the situation and embracing its truth. The client will be less susceptible to strong and protracted unpleasant emotions if they practice radical acceptance without passing judgment or trying to reject reality. There are four skill areas in the module on distress tolerance:

- Distracting
- Self-soothing
- Enhancing the present
- Concentrating on advantages and disadvantages

These abilities are meant to assist people in handling hardship and times of crisis without ignoring it or making it worse. Use the worksheets from this chapter and assist your kids to develop distress tolerance.

Quote Wall

Whenever kids feel angry, ask them to write their favorite quote on this wall.

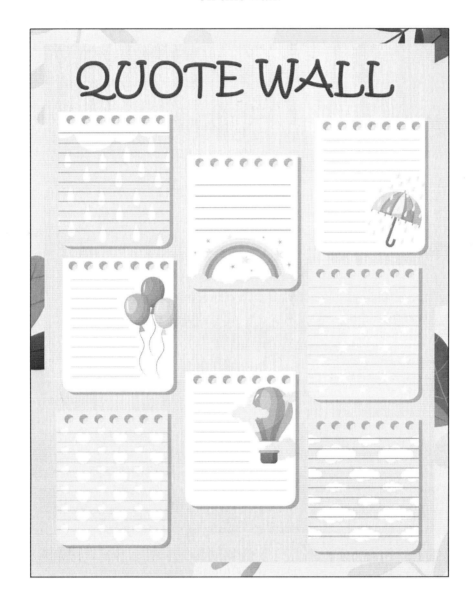

Failing Forward

For Parents - For most parents, failing forward—the concept of using mistakes as a springboard for learning and development—is a formidable talent.

We have a propensity as a society to emphasize success alone. Failure is often viewed as something to be embarrassed by or to fear, but failing forward is about embracing our mistakes as stepping stones to success. Parents need to be exceptionally adept at this skill.

Failing forward for parents entails letting their kids deal with the unavoidable effects of their choices. Instead of having your child bring their homework to school, you should let them take the poor rating for not turning it in on time if they forgot their assignment because they were disorganized or couldn't prepare the night before. They will be internally motivated to prepare themselves better the next time due to that "failure."

In this case, instead of criticizing your child for being disorganized, you should ask them how it felt not to have their schoolwork prepared and how they felt about receiving a lesser grade. Parents may say that the internal sense of struggle will produce a stronger incentive to be more prepared the next time. Young people are also allowed to learn from their errors, which will benefit them in the long run.

By embracing failure as a chance for growth, failing forward removes the fear associated with failure. It is an excellent method for assisting children in managing stress and anxiety since it removes expectations from the majority of circumstances and teaches your child that failure does not equate to personal failure and that progress is always possible.

Moment to Pause

Pausing for a moment is an essential DBT skill because DBT focuses on understanding how your body reacts to stress and developing internal systems to recognize and reroute stress or irritation in healthy ways.

Allowing yourself or your kid a time to breathe, stepping back from a circumstance, and deciding how to proceed are the main points of pausing. This is referred to as "going to your corners" in certain families.

This ability focuses on identifying when an argument or scenario is becoming too heated, and emotions are beginning to rise. Recognizing the circumstance and deciding to leave the area until everyone has calmed down is what it means to pause for a moment. The idea of pausing is easy to understand but challenging to implement.

Parents can use this ability to assist and teach their children how to manage stress and anxiety by giving their children a code word. Imagine, for instance, that two siblings are engaged in a contentious discussion that soon develops into a fight when someone shouts, "Code red!" Everyone agrees to end the disagreement as soon as it is mentioned and must be sent to separate rooms for a while to cool off, giving the siblings some distance from the issue that led to fight.

Even though it might be challenging to understand and practice, taking a moment to halt is perhaps one of the most beneficial life lessons you can teach your children.

The 12 Tools

Here are twelve important tools to enhance distress tolerance skills. Help your kids to develop all these tools one by one.

GIVE

GIVE

Gentle

Accept the NO's you might get. Don't react by attacking or getting angry.

Interested

Show interest by being a good listener. This means no interrupting.

Validate

Restate the other persons' feelings and what they are saying. Respect their thoughts and opinions.

Easy

Smile, relax your shoulders, act in a light-hearted and easy way.

Personal Crisis Plan

Help kids to customize their crisis plan.

PERSONAL CRISIS PLAN

I know I'm triggered when I notice

_____
_____
_____

SOME GOOD WAYS TO DISTRACT MYSELF ARE:

SAFE People I Can Reach Out To:

1. _____
2. _____
3. _____

Coping Skills I Can Use:

Ways To Keep Myself & My Space Safe:

_____
_____
_____

Others Resources I Can Use To Get Myself Care

1.
2.
3.

The Best Dream

This fun activity will help your kids in stressed times.

Name My Anxiety

Coping Toolbox

Coping Tool Box

Date:

1. Identify 1-5 Triggers

2. Identify 1-5 Warning Signs

4. Identify 1-5 strengths about yourself.

3. Identify 1-5 Coping Techniques

Daily Self-Reflection

Daily Self-Reflection

Date:

1. What is one thing you are most grateful for today?

2. What was your biggest highlight from today?

3. What was one challenge you experienced today?

4. What is at least one thing you learned from that challenge?

5. What is one goal you plan to accomplish tomorrow?

Growth Mindset

Help kids to identify positive and negative thoughts. Complete the worksheet.

Name: _____

GROWTH MINDSET
What Can I Say to Myself?

Instead of...	Try thinking...
I'm not good at this.	What am I missing?
I'm awesome at this.	I'm on the right track.
I give up.	I'll use some of the strategies we've learned.
This is too hard.	
I can't make this any better.	
I just can't do math, (or reading, or social studies, or writing, or science...)	
I made a mistake.	
She's so smart. I'll never be that smart.	
It's good enough.	
Plan A didn't work.	

In or Out of Control

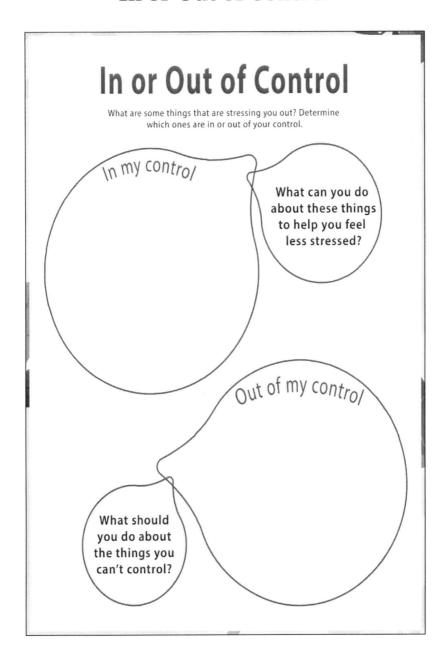

My Calm Down Tricks

My Calm Down Tricks

1. Go outside and kick a ball or run around.

2. Punch a pillow.

3. Listen to music or sing a song.

4. Close your eyes and think of a calm place.

5. Draw a picture.

6. Write a letter or a story.

7. Read a book.

8. Talk to someone.

9. Ask for a hug.

Stress in my Day

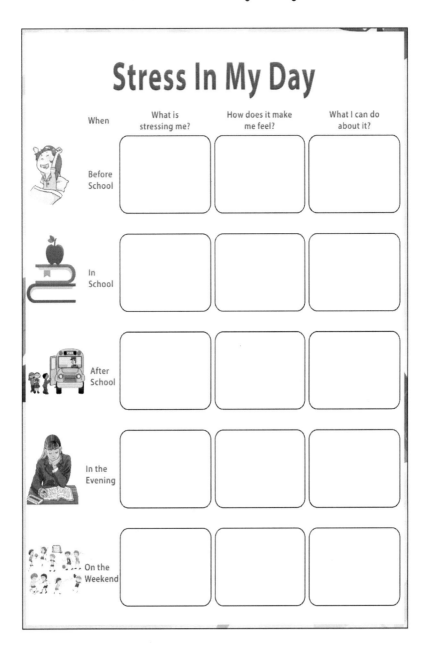

Stress In My Day

When	What is stressing me?	How does it make me feel?	What I can do about it?
Before School			
In School			
After School			
In the Evening			
On the Weekend			

Chapter 4: Mindfulness

The important technique emphasized in DBT is mindfulness because it is incredibly difficult to alter ingrained emotional, cognitive, and behavioral habits without awareness.

Controlling emotions, navigating crises without things getting worse, and amicably resolving interpersonal issues all depend on mindfulness.

Engaging your Smart Mind, another fundamental DBT idea also requires mindfulness.

Eastern meditative techniques are used in the cognitive behavior therapy branch known as dialectical behavior therapy (DBT). The DBT philosophy's central principle, the synthesis of extremes, especially acceptance and change, is where the dialectic originates. We believe that we are all capable of change and growth and that we are all good enough as we are. These two ideas could appear to be at odds with one another, but we can comprehend these seemingly incompatible realities side by side, thanks to the compelling conversation or dialectic.

DBT is taught as a set of abilities in four modules: distress tolerance, emotional control, interpersonal effectiveness, and mindfulness. Core mindfulness, the first of these modules, is the cornerstone of DBT, as its name suggests. Western contemplative practices and philosophy are at the core of mindfulness. Being mindful means being aware of your thoughts, feelings, actions, and urges to act. We gain the ability to take control of our lives in a new way by developing our mindfulness. It has been established that awareness helps with emotional control. We accept and modify ourselves as we come to terms with who we are. It involves paying attention and setting goals. States of mind are the foundational idea of core mindfulness in DBT. Mindfulness activities will help your kids to stay calm and stress-free all day.

Ride the Wave

A surfer rides the wave's natural tide rather than opposing the huge ocean wave. A psychological technique is known as "riding the wave" which involves surfing your own strong, negative emotions. The acceptance of negative emotions like grief and rage is delayed by fighting against them. Letting your emotions be there without acting ineffectively is what it means to "ride the wave." You'll return to a position of tranquility rather than emotional upheaval, like a rising tide coming and disappearing.

Your emotions alter in the same way that ocean waves do. Your feelings might be quiet and pleasant one second and rocky and unexpected the next, just like waves. When under stress, a person may exhibit emotional restlessness, also referred to as dysregulation, and attempt to manage their strong emotions in a negative or ineffective way, which may worsen the situation and lead the person to disregard long-term priorities, goals, and values. It is difficult to regulate and manage strong emotions when you become dysregulated.

You can feel overwhelmed and overtaken by negative emotions and cravings. As the feelings are too intense to handle, there might be a sense of hopelessness. Riding the wave is useful in this situation. Urge surfing, also known as riding the wave, is accepting the experience as it is without trying to alter it. It may feel odd to ride the wave and stay with the discomfort because the urge is more often to have an escape from the problem. A surfer rides a wave until it reaches its natural end by going with the flow.

Accepting our ideas and controlling our emotions can be difficult, but if we can learn to ride the wave, we can stop our urges from controlling our actions. Understanding that we have power over our conduct and have learned how to make informed decisions to improve productivity in our daily lives might give us a greater sense of security.

Square Breathing

Count and follow breath pattern given below.

Mindful Posing

Body poses are a simple method for kids to start practicing mindfulness. Inform your children that striking amusing positions can make them feel courageous, strong, and pleased to get them thrilled.

Send the youngsters to a calm, recognizable location where they can feel secure. Then, request them to attempt one of these poses:

The Superman position is performed by standing with the feet slightly wider than the hips, the fists clenched, and the arms extended as high as possible.

Standing tall and spreading your legs broader than hip-width apart, strike the Wonder Woman posture by placing your hands or fists on your hips.

After a few repetitions of either of these stances, ask the children how they feel. You might be amazed with the results.

Spidey-Senses

This can be a connected "next step" to teach youngsters how to stay in the moment while discussing superheroes.

Give your children instructions on how to activate their "Spidey senses," or the hyper-focused senses of smell, vision, sound, tasting, and touch that Spiderman employs to monitor his environment. This will nudge them to halt and concentrate on the present, making them more aware of the data their senses are bringing in.

This traditional mindfulness exercise promotes curiosity and observation, two excellent human qualities to practice.

The Mindful Jar

Children can learn through this practice how powerful emotions can take control and how to calm down when they seem overwhelming.

First, grab a clear container (such as a Mason jar) and almost fill it with water. Then, fill the jar with a generous amount of glitter glue or glue and dried glitter. To make the glitter and glue mixture, put the jar's lid and shake it.

Finally, create your mini-lesson or drawing inspiration from it.

"Consider the glitter a representation of your agitated, angry, or upset thoughts. Observe how they spin about and seriously impair your vision. Because you can't think properly while irritated, making stupid decisions is simple. Do not be alarmed; this is common and affects everyone.

[At this point, place the jar in front of kids.]

Now observe what transpires after a short period of stillness. Continue to look. Watch as the water becomes clearer and the glitter begins to settle. You have the same mental processes. Your mind begins to quiet down, and you begin to see things much more clearly after a short period of calm. When going through this delicate process, taking deep breaths can help us relax.

Children can practice mindfulness while concentrating on the spinning glitter in the jar through this activity, which also teaches them how emotions can affect the way they think.

Take Five

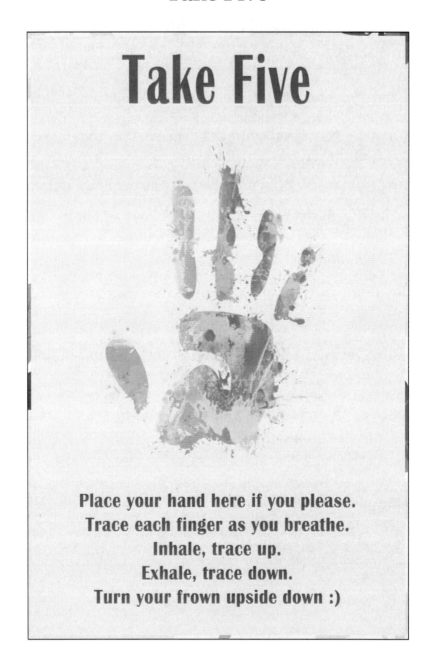

Take Five

Place your hand here if you please.
Trace each finger as you breathe.
Inhale, trace up.
Exhale, trace down.
Turn your frown upside down :)

Safari

The Safari activity is a fantastic approach to teaching youngsters mindfulness. An ordinary walk becomes a thrilling new adventure, thanks to this activity.

Assert that you are going on a safari, and your children's task is to spot as many birds, insects, creepy-crawlies, and other creatures as possible. They will need to concentrate on all of their skills to find them, particularly smaller ones, as everything that walks, creeps, jumps, or flies is interesting.

The mindfulness walk is a similar adult workout. Children respond to this activity in the same way that adults respond to a mindful walk: they become more aware and present.

Five Finger Breathing

A mindfulness exercise is known as "five-finger breathing" which teaches kids to pause and take five slow breaths using their fingers. This activity is particularly helpful when kids don't have access to the tools that make up a mindfulness toolbox because it can be done anywhere, at any time. Additionally, it enables kids to feel grounded, stay in the moment, and handle strong emotions.

- Start by setting one hand on the floor or in front of you.
- Your fingers should be apart.
- As you take a deep breath, start tracing up the outside of the thumb with the pointer finger of the other hand.
- As you exhale, trace the thumb's interior.
- Be sure to breathe in as you draw up the finger and trace down as you do this for the other fingers.
- After that, take a moment to consider your feelings, then repeat as necessary.

Nature Yoga Poses

Here are some easy and fun yoga poses for kids.

VRIKSASANA POSE

Trees are a tremendous source of inspiration when it comes to 'grounding' yoga poses. This posture mirrors a tree's delicate and stable stance. Unlike most yoga postures, this one requires you to keep your eyes open. If you constantly perform this stance, you will quickly see that you have:

- Improved leg stability and balance
- Legs with extra muscle and strength
- An increase in pelvic stability
- Enhancing the health of your leg and hip bones
- Greater assurance and self-worth

MONTANAGE POSE

The Montanage posture is great for "grounding" since it helps you feel solid and unmoving. Like many yoga postures, this one has many health advantages, including better posture, strengthening of the knees, elbows, and ankles, toning of the buttocks and abs, relief from sciatica, and a reduction in flat feet. The list is endless! Whether it serves as a starting pose, a resting pose, or a tool to enhance posture, you should include this pose in your subsequent practice. Get barefoot and feel the soft grass under your feet to deepen your connection with nature.

POSE CORPSE

This one is the easiest stance to perform but the most difficult to perfect. Although you appear to be dozing off in the pose, the goal is to be completely relaxed and conscious simultaneously. This is why the pose is so challenging to perfect. Make sure you are comfortable while lying on your back, and then take a deep breath to signal to your body that you will be ready to relax. Check your muscles for tension while performing this pose, and make an effort to put distracting thoughts to rest.

- When you have it down, you can profit from:
- Headache reduction
- Decreases hypertension
- Enhance fatigue and sleeplessness
- Improved concentration and relaxation

Flower Breathing

Flower Breathing

Slowly trace the flower petals.

breathe out

breathe in

breathe in

breathe out

Start at the star.
Breathe in for 2 petals.
Breathe out for 2 petals.

Feather Breathing

Feather Breathing

How to:

- Collect different coloured feathers.

- Ask your child to hold the feather in their hand.

- Take a deep breath. {Model this for your child}

- To help kids learn how to take a deep breath, ask them to put their hands on their bellies and feel the rise and fall.

- Inhale slowly for a count of 3 - 1,2,3..

- Then. slowly exhale through the nose and while exhaling blow gently up one side of the feather and down the other side.

Mindfulness Bingo

Try these activities and mark them. Go in straight lines (from up to down or left to right) while marking.

Mindfulness Bingo

Mindful journaling	Nostril swap breathing	Gratitude list	Mindful pinwheel breathing	Mindful melt
Mindful Play-Ooh squeeze	Mindful shoulder roll	Mindful breathing	Mindful gardening	Mindful bottle
Mindful patience	Mindful car ride	Free Space	Mindful sound observation	Mindful sand flow
Mindful nature work	Squeeze and go	Mindful house walk	Mindful yoga	Body scan
Mindful eating	Mindful music	Mindful object focus	Mindful teeth brushing	Acknowledge and accept feelings

Mindfulness Drawings

When your kids feel down, give them colors and these pages. These drawings help relaxing mind and body.

Mindfulness Drawings

Bunny Breathing

Bunny Breathing

Breathing Strategy

1. Pretend to be a bunny holding a carrot.

2. Sniff air in with your nose 3 times to smell the carrot.
(1 sniff, 2 sniff, 3 sniff)

3. Breathe air out slowly through your nose and relax.
(1 slow breath)

Calm Down Yoga

To calm down your kids, try these poses.

Mindfulness Games

Here are several interactive activities for kids.

Creating Bubbles: Encourage your children to concentrate on inhaling slowly and deeply and steadily exhaling to fill the bubble. Encourage children to observe the bubbles as they appear, separate, pop, or drift away.

Pinwheels. Use the same strategies as when blowing bubbles to promote conscious attention on the pinwheels.

Balloon-Related Play. Have your children move slowly and softly while explaining that the game's object is to keep the balloon off the ground. If it helps, you can instruct them to act like the balloon is delicate.

Texture Pouch. Put several small, distinctively textured, or shaped things in a bag. Have each youngster one at a time, reach inside and touch an item while describing their feelings. Make sure they don't remove the item from the bag, leaving them with only their hands to examine it.

Blindfolded taste evaluations. Put a blindfold on each youngster and ask them to simulate their first time eating a small meal, such as a raisin or a cranberry.

The Bottom Line

Today's kids deal with anxiety too frequently. Younger grade-schoolers might not be able to properly comprehend or articulate their own sensations when it relates to childhood anxiety. Although there is no assurance that older children will tell you what is upsetting them, they may be able to explain it to you. It will be easier for you to see issues before they negatively affect your child if you are aware of changes in their behavior.

The goal of DBT for kids is to help your child recognize their special place in the world. It is a very successful approach. Your kid is free to be wholly himself in a welcoming, secure setting. Being sensitive does not necessarily indicate a problem. It is just a new means of getting about.

Your youngster will enter this setting to have their needs acknowledged. They will learn how to alter their actions to make life a little simpler through sessions centered on acceptance and reinforcement punishment. This is a type of child and family counseling, unlike other types of DBT programs for various age groups. Your active involvement as a parent is essential to your child's long-term development.

You will first get the opportunity to learn about your child's experiences. We will next concentrate on creating new coping strategies for next chapters in order to help create the accepting atmosphere your child needs in order to make their own positive transformation. To teach your child that acting out will not get them attention, this book will teach them how to ignore the disruptive behavior. This is crucial for building a trustworthy relationship and allowing your child the chance to commit to the upcoming work. So, give these activities to your kids and help them to control their emotions and feelings.

Made in United States
North Haven, CT
24 June 2023

38180284R10061